The Secret of Design Effectiveness

Newell and Sorrell

Acknowledgements

We are grateful to all our clients and their representatives who are named in this book. Without their help, including the provision of information and figures for the original submissions to DBA Design Effectiveness Awards, this book would not have been possible. And very special thanks to Caroline Wilson!

Photography/Illustration

The Body Shop *Robert Voke*; Boots *Richard Prescott*; Routledge *Fi McGhee*; Berol *Richard Foster*; Niceday *Charles Barsotti*; InterCity *Richard Foster*; Bloomsbury *Barbera Decher*; Royal Mail *Simon Wright.*

Printed by Penshurst Press on Envirocote (McNaughton Paper).

Newell and Sorrell UK

4 Utopia Village Chalcot Road London NW1 8LH United Kingdom
Telephone +44 (0)171 722 1113
Facsimile +44 (0)171 722 0259
ISDN +44 (0)171 722 6988
E mail n+s-utop@online.rednet.co.uk

Newell and Sorrell Nederland

MGR Van de Weteringstraat 132E 3581 En Utrecht Nederland
Telefoon +31(0)30 302 802
Facsimile +31(0)30 367 501
ISDN +31 (0)30 300 864

Contents

The bottom line and the high ground

by John Sorrell

Design effectiveness is one of the best kept commercial secrets. Too few organisations know the true value of effective design, and the facts and figures are not often revealed. Yet effective design can achieve an extraordinary range of business objectives.

Effective design is design that makes a difference. It enhances the performance of organisations, and adds value to the products and services they provide for customers. It gives competitive edge. It creates wealth and prosperity, and improves the quality of life. Significantly, it operates on more than one level.

Design effectiveness influences the bottom line for any company. Of this, there can be no doubt, as the facts and figures contained in this book demonstrate. Increases in turnover, sales, profits and market share are tangible benefits which result from effective design investment. But effective design also enables organisations to occupy the high ground in terms of forging an ethical and socially responsible relationship with staff and customers, and in suffusing all transactions with quality.

So design effectiveness has a dual meaning. It certainly means making more money, but also much more besides. It represents an investment in broadening knowledge and in the future. Take, for example, one of the case studies described here: the creation of a new approach to boost entries from schools to the Royal Mail's annual letter-writing competition. How do you put a bottom-line value on that?

The design effectiveness of that project went beyond the reflex issue of a financial return to tap deep roots in our society, although the Royal Mail's cost-effective investment in its school-age consumers of tomorrow also made sound commercial sense.

My point is that the bottom line and the high ground are spokes of the same wheel in the fully-rounded argument for design effectiveness. They are linked in the same way that companies with a tangible competitive edge can create wealth for their staff and investors.

In this process, design plays an important role because it makes ideas accessible. It is only when people inside an organisation start using design effectively that the future becomes visible. The founder directors of Bloomsbury Publishing, for example, had only ambition, broad ideas and start-up finance before they came to Newell and Sorrell to create an identity that would define the precise qualities of their new, radically different imprint.

Of course, some people say that the exact contribution of design to the effectiveness of any strategy or project is difficult to measure - and if you can't measure it mathematically, you shouldn't use it because you don't know how useful it can be. I accept that the design industry still has some way to go to perfect the monitoring mechanisms and evaluation tools to measure design effectiveness properly. However, we are steadily getting there and imperfect tracking techniques should be no excuse for companies to deny themselves this most potent of marketing and development disciplines. One of the purposes of publishing this book is to stimulate greater debate and research into the whole issue of design effectiveness and, indeed, to initiate a literature in this under-documented area of business.

There is, however, a dichotomy in analysing the effectiveness of design that we must confront. To measure the role of design, it must be *isolated* from other activities such as advertising, PR or technology. Yet for design to be most effective, it must be integrated with adjacent disciplines to give any new strategy or launch the best chance of success.

I want to see design measured properly, but I don't want to see it isolated from other disciplines. I regard the creative process as a concurrent process from beginning to end, with design an integral part of the marketing and development mix.

The growing credibility of the Design Effectiveness Awards scheme, run by the Design Business Association, is helping to get this message across to business and industry - and I am proud of Newell and Sorrell's record in winning six awards in the short time since the inauguration of this scheme, judged by senior business managers.

Those Design Effectiveness Awards winners are included in this publication which draws on eight case studies of projects undertaken by Newell and Sorrell. These case studies, written by different consultants in Newell and Sorrell, show the many different ways in which effective design can support corporate objectives. It can reach new markets, as in the case of Berol's move into the quality art-graphics market, or The Body Shop's mail order expansion into America, or the spectacular penetration of the UK baby food and drink market by Boots.

It can unite the organisation, as in the identities for Routledge and Niceday which provided the rallying flag for organisations formed by the merger of several different companies. It can reposition the brand, as in the case of InterCity which became the profitable flagship of British Rail. It can launch a new venture, as in the case of Bloomsbury Publishing, or raise awareness as with the Royal Mail and its letter-writing competition.

Some of the evidence of effectiveness is in the form of hard business data. Some is more anecdotal. Both are relevant. It is a cliché but there is no escaping the fact that design is a 'people business'. Quotations from people can encapsulate the success of a particular enterprise, like the customer of Niceday office supplies who, in a commodity purchasing sector, remarked: "The cartoons cheer up the products - they make you smile."

What matters to me is that design should make a difference - to the way people feel, to the way they behave, *to the bottom line and to the high ground.*

Hello America!

by Frances Newell

The Body Shop wanted to enter the US market and secure its trademark across the States without over-stretching itself financially by opening stores nationwide. Newell and Sorrell created the mail order catalogues that introduced this unique corporate culture to the USA.

I had been aware of Anita Roddick for a long time. Everyone had, at least in the UK. Observing her from the outside, I admired what she was doing with The Body Shop. Here was a company with an idea, and it conveyed that idea in a way that was very clear and very commercial.

  Anita is a great collector. She is famous for travelling the world and coming back with exotic ingredients for new products. I suppose her initial approach to Newell and Sorrell had something of the same spirit. She had seen our work and I think that what appealed to her was a sense of intelligent commercialism. Whatever it was, John Sorrell and I were invited down to Littlehampton to meet Anita and talk about a new project.

There is no doubt that The Body Shop is a missionary company, a company that wears its beliefs openly. Long before green credentials became fashionable in retailing, The Body Shop had made passionate concern for the environment a key part of its corporate ethos. During the 1980s the company embraced issues such as ozone depletion, the commercial exploitation of animals and destruction of the rain forests.

It seems clear to me that this sharp focus on a vision is a fundamental requirement for a successful company. Effective design will come from enabling such a vision to shine out and be seen by different audiences. Sometimes we have to create a vision; sometimes the fog of history makes it difficult to do so. But with The Body Shop there was no such problem. The Body Shop remained a commercial concern with a conscience - highly profitable, with an expanding network of shops, and with a charismatic leader.

The next logical step for the business was to break into the large and potentially profitable American market. This was the new project that Anita Roddick talked to us about.

Establishing a bridgehead in America is not easy. Many

British companies have tried and failed. There is the danger of financial over-commitment above all. Anxious to avoid this, The Body Shop had established two initial outlets to gain a foothold in the US market, one in New York and another in New Jersey.

Subsequently it was decided that a mail order operation would be the most effective way for The Body Shop to boost its American growth without over-reaching itself.

To generate US public interest in the proposed mail order operation, a public relations programme was launched in 1988 with Anita Roddick's personal involvement at its heart. This led to Newell and Sorrell's first involvement, and we designed *Hello America,* a PR profile. This introduced The Body Shop concept to the American public by generating editorial coverage in the media.

The success of this strategy - particularly a profile of Anita in *People* magazine - resulted in considerable public interest in The Body Shop's mail order venture. The next step was to produce the catalogue.

Two pragmatic considerations lay behind The Body Shop's decision to launch a mail order operation in the United States. First, postal trading across the country would enable the company to protect its trademark in every state, since under American law a trademark may only be secured in states where the owner actually trades. Second, the mail order option avoided the administrative and financial problems of opening a large number of retail outlets across the country.

Despite these advantages, the need to sell The Body Shop's products effectively whilst still projecting its unique corporate culture remained a high priority. Without retail outlets, the task of capturing the essence of The Body Shop and selling it off the mail order catalogue page to middle America was going to be a challenge.

The catalogue had to be like the shop in printed form. It had to look like The Body Shop, it had to convey that eclectic mix of colours, graphics, ingredients and do so with honesty. We were committed to using recycled paper, not an easy commitment when accurate colour reproduction was an essential element of the catalogue. However, we worked closely with paper manufacturers and printers, we did test after test, in the end achieving the quality we wanted.

This was important not just to make a 'green' point but because we knew the catalogue had to sell - and how could you sell cosmetics properly if the colours did not match reality?

Integrity was the key focus. Anita Roddick wants The Body Shop to be the most honest cosmetics company around. She introduced the mail order catalogue by writing: "People today want honest information. We do not create false needs through advertising. We tell the story behind what we sell and what our customers buy. And The Body Shop story is here for all to see in this catalogue".

Initial results exceeded all expectations. The catalogue was a phenomenal success. In mid 1989, 100,000 copies of the catalogue were printed in the UK and delivered to the USA for distribution. An opening mailing list of 20,000 was established and the immediate response was unprecedented: in just two months US sales of Body Shop products more than trebled.

We were immediately asked to update the catalogue with an additional print run of 100,000. By the end of 1989 almost 150,000 catalogues had been mailed and Body Shop business during this period doubled, with average individual orders increasing from around $25 to $30.

Together these two mailings generated a response rate of nearly 20 per cent - unprecedented in the US mail order industry.

The mail order catalogue opened up the US market to The Body Shop, in a way that accurately embodied the company's style and culture. The catalogue itself became an expression of green principles, making new converts for the environmental cause as well as winning new customers for The Body Shop.

Subsequent versions of the catalogue built upon the success, and as more Body Shop retail outlets opened in America, the catalogue fulfilled an additional valuable role in increasing market share and defending against the competition.

Anita Roddick wrote: "Through the mail order catalogue we aimed to reach an even wider audience in the USA. We were determined to do it in our own way, tapping into the common thread of humanity that is part of our appeal. The US mail order catalogue expressed so vividly what The Body Shop is. And of course in business terms it has been phenomenally successful".

Perhaps the real success is shown by some final figures. In 1989 The Body Shop had two US retail outlets. *At the beginning of 1995 it had over 200.*

Key facts

* Gross sales trebled as a result of an initial mailing to 20,000 people

* Response rate to the next 150,000 mailing was an unprecedented 20%

* 70 - 80% of the customer base re-ordered at least once

* Over 5% ordered up to 5 times in 6 months

* Total sales in the initial 10 month period was $965,921

WINNER Design Effectiveness Award for Consumer Literature

"Through the mail order catalogue we aimed to reach an even wider audience in the USA ... in business terms it has been phenomenally successful."

Anita Roddick The Body Shop

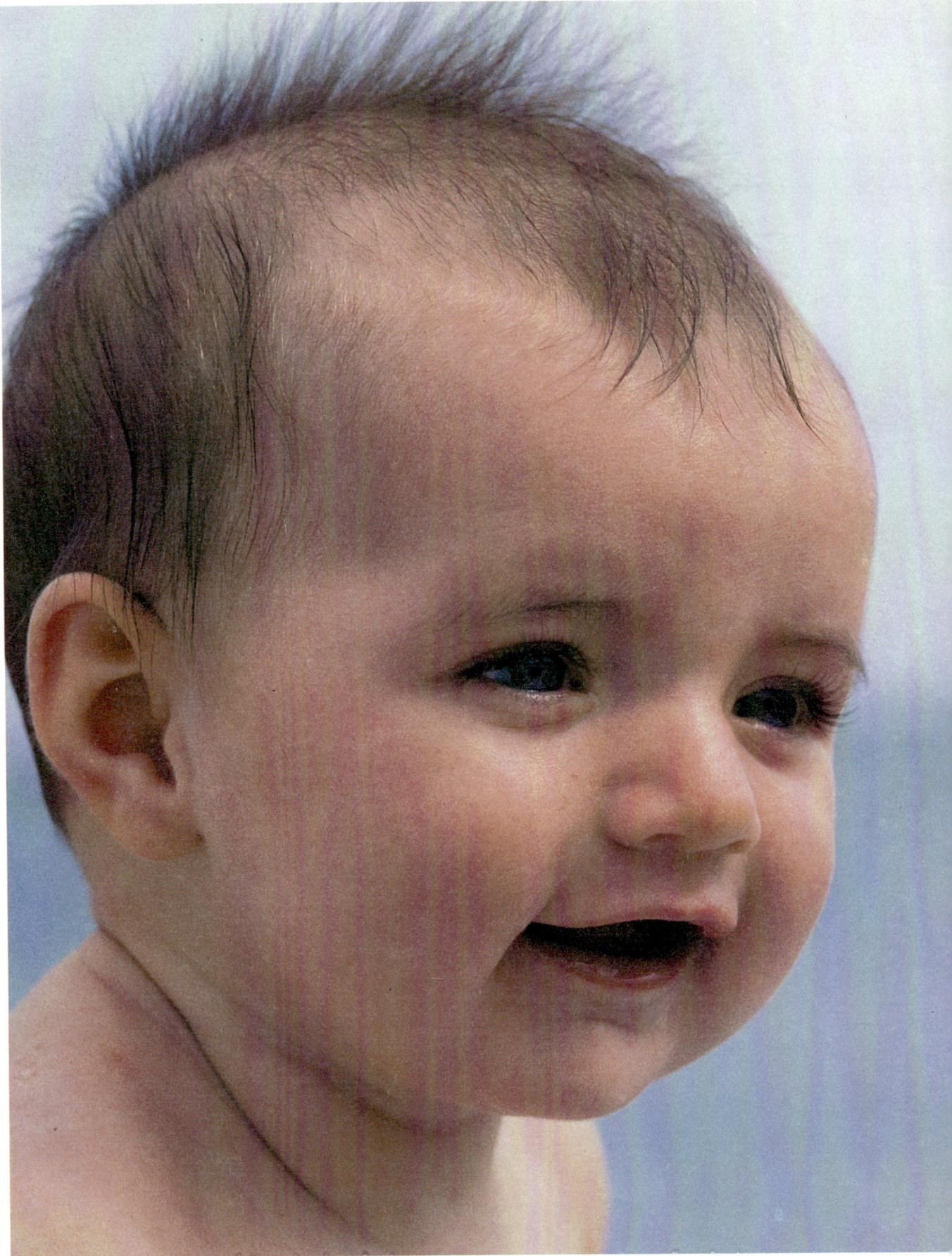

Baby boom

by Jeremy Scholfield

The Boots range of baby foods grew from small beginnings to capture a large share of the market. Newell and Sorrell created the brand identity and packaging which helped Boots increase its sales six-fold in three years.

You have to admire Boots for the clarity of its brand. It speaks to customers in the reassuring tones of 'the man in the white coat'. Drawing authority from its roots as Boots the Chemists, all the product categories and own-brand products in Boots stores benefit from the overall values of the brand.

We had worked with Boots for some time on many different product ranges when we were asked to look at the baby food and drink range. This would be a part of a programme to strengthen the overall proposition of Boots as the 0-5 specialist. Over the years our respect for the brand had grown, and so had Boots' own confidence in what had been a previously undervalued asset. Respect breeds confidence and both qualities encourage mutual trust. Respect, confidence and trust communicate to customers. A partnership based on these qualities is a solid foundation for effective design.

When we started, the task seemed anything but easy. Here we were in the early 1990s with recession hitting everyone hard. The birthrate had declined; family disposable income was shrinking. As a result baby food manufacturers started to cut prices.

Boots had entered the baby food market trading on its reputation for quality and reliability. By 1990 market share stood at 2 per cent. Boots decided to expand its market share through a brand development programme with a packaging redesign at its core.

Alan Wilson was the Boots Group Product Manager, who stated: "Boots brand range of baby foods lacked an identity to link a comprehensive product range across a number of diverse baby food sectors."

There were a number of problems that emerged from the comprehensive review we undertook. Baby food itself looks unappetising - at least to adults - so we decided to focus on the ingredients which are healthy and appetising. We decided to concentrate on presenting Boots as a serious retailer, relying on simplicity and clarity. Above all, we went for a quality of photography that beat anything else around.

In other words, we reinforced the core values of the Boots brand. We recognised that the brand had enormous authority, and we used it.

The ranges we designed - sub-brands, if you like - were made up of a standard range as well as premium products which sold at premium prices. Here the strategy was quite different from the own-brand norm. There was nothing basic about the products, the brand or the packaging.

Eventually, we designed 150-plus products across four ranges, creating an overall brand identity in the baby food area. Our design approach emphasised healthy ingredients and nutritional benefits for the standard range. We then worked on two premium sub-brands which built additional values on the solid foundation we had laid.

The first range was Mother's Recipe, which guarantees that 95 per cent of vegetables used in the 25 products in the range are organically produced. This was the first organic range in the UK, breaking fresh ground. The second range was First Harvest, which uses atmospheric photography in its 40 products to convey the use of fine ingredients grown using traditional farming methods.

Certain features were critical to all three ranges. Information was reorganised to be more consumer-friendly. Photography was of the highest quality, making the ingredients look mouth-watering. These qualities linked to the reassuring endorsement of the Boots brand so that mothers could sense authority, expertise, value, trust.

The impact on sales was immediate. From a sales base of £2 million and a market share of 2 per cent in 1991, sales of Boots baby foods rose dramatically. In 1992 sales grew to £6.4 million, giving Boots a market share of 5.9 per cent. In 1993 sales rose again, up to £10.1 million with a market share of 8.5 per cent. By 1994 sales stood at £13.1 million, and Boots share of the £121 million baby food market was 10.8 per cent.

The premium sub-brands performed well in their own right, Mother's Recipe winning a 1 per cent share of the national baby food market, and First Harvest achieving sales of £2.1 million and a 5 per cent share in its first year since launch in 1993.

The effect on perceptions inside Boots was noticeable. As the challenge to brands such as Cow & Gate's Olvarit became more and more effective, pride in their own brand

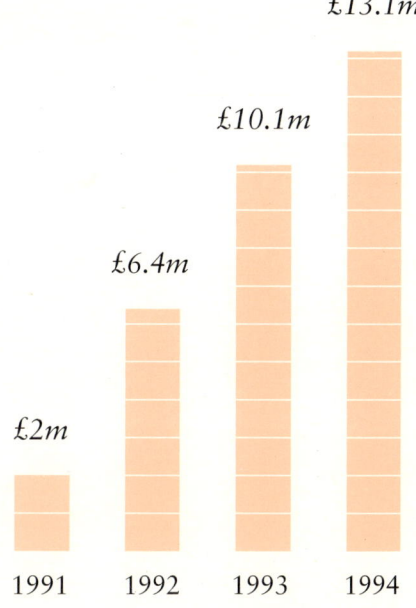

£13.1m

£10.1m

£6.4m

£2m

1991   1992   1993   1994

Increase in sales 1991-1994

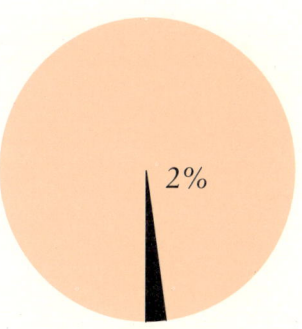

2%

Boots market share
of Baby Foods in 1991

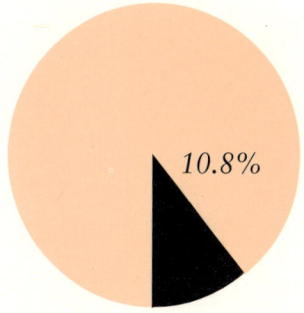

10.8%

Boots market share
of Baby Foods in 1994

was reinforced among Boots managers. The overall share of Boots baby food products sold in-store has grown from 15 to 45 per cent. You also have to set this achievement in context. Cow & Gate and Heinz, for example, have built brand awareness through years of mainstream consumer advertising, whereas the advertising spend on Boots baby food has been more low key - with an impactful TV and and colour press campaign for First Harvest on launch in May 1993.

Boots Product Manager Justine Squitieri put it like this : "All Boots brand products must show empathy with our customers and communicate our expertise in fulfilling their requirements." That was our aim with the branding and packaging we carried out. The brand supports the sub-brand, the sub-brand supports the brand. *It seems like a winning formula.*

Key facts

The new Boots baby food brand identity achieved:

* Sales increase from around £2 million in 1991 to £13.1 million in 1994

* An increase in market share from 2% to 10.8%

* The largest sales increase by any baby food manufacturer

* A jump from 15% to 45% in Boots Brand share of in-store sales

WINNER Design Effectiveness Award for Own Brand Food & Drink Packaging

"The excellent redesign work and the launch of a number of innovative products has resulted in outstanding value and share growth for the Boots range of baby foods."

Alan Wilson
Boots *Group Product Manager*

Four into one will go

by John Simmons

Routledge was created by merging four publishing houses. Initially the merger generated little excitement. Newell and Sorrell created a new corporate identity which unified the company, simplified design management and boosted sales.

I have always loved books. My degree was in English Literature and my working life began in publishing. I believe, with Shelley, that 'poets are the unacknowledged legislators of the world'.

I give you these facts because there is no doubt that enthusiasm can contribute an enormous amount to design effectiveness. If you not only *understand* but also *love* the client's products, you really are able to add value. The best design shines with the emotion and commitment that have been poured into it.

Effective design also needs a good client. When I first met David Croom of Routledge, it became clear that we were on the same wavelength. David had very clear objectives for what he wanted to do; I understood what he was trying to do and knew that we would be able to help him.

The situation was that Routledge had been formed by a merger between four publishing houses owned by International Thomson. The constituent companies - Routledge & Kegan Paul, Methuen Academic, Tavistock and Croom Helm - were known in their particular areas of expertise, but the aim was to create a single strong company which would become a major player in the academic book market.

The first eighteen months of the new company had passed, and there was no real sign that Routledge was making its presence felt in the market. There was a credibility gap, internally and externally. Loyalty to the old imprints lingered on. A new logo, designed in-house, had done little by itself to motivate staff or improve external perceptions.

David Croom decided that a new corporate identity was needed to achieve a number of objectives. First, there was the need to project clearly Routledge's unity and sense of purpose. A strong identity would support the marketing of current titles and attract design as a competitive tool that could be used to set Routledge apart from its competitors.

The foundation for the programme that now began was a series of interviews with key people in Routledge. People had talked about the 'robber barons', meaning that the four publishing groups (based on the old imprints) had loyalties to themselves rather than to the overall company. The important thing was to show that everybody would gain by working to the shared objectives exemplified by the new identity.

There was widespread concern, for example, about the way that design was managed. Books and book jackets were churned out like sausages. After all, there were 600 books published a year and the design department had only three people in it. Yet each book published should look as if it deserves to be published. Each book should look cared for.

"Why," we asked "do academic books have to look boring?"

There is no good reason why. There is every reason why they should look challenging, interesting and, when gathered together, should present an impression of coherence and authority.

The visual elements of the new identity encompassed a logotype, colours, typefaces, the use of photography and illustration and the introduction of an identifying pattern. We surprised Routledge too by helping them to improve areas that they had not considered as coming within the realms of identity. For example, we gave them a new focus on the words used to promote their books. A system for writing blurbs - involving the use of questions leading into a shorter blurb - directed attention to the question "How will we best sell this book?"

The visual elements were simple enough. The logotype was an evolution from the version that had been developed in-house - the new version incorporated the company name as an integral part of the design, making it suitable for use on front jackets and spines. Black and white were used predominantly, allowing any other colours to be combined on individual books without compromising the strength of the publisher's visual identity on the shelves.

But in many ways the most important visual element was the one that initially aroused the most puzzlement: the use of a pattern strip on book jackets, stationery and promotional material. The pattern itself was based on an Islamic device and it gave an elegant framework and point of distinction to Routledge books. It also became, as we had hoped, a playful element of the identity. As people became accustomed to it, they began to explore its potential and to use it in decorative ways. Visual enjoyment entered the corporate bloodstream.

In this way the identity changed the personality of the company as well as the appearance of the products. The formerly beleaguered design department gained new authority and job satisfaction. In line with our recommendations the department increased in size; it also increased in quality because recruits were attracted by Routledge's new approach. Staff turnover throughout the company reduced, while productivity and morale increased.

These were measurable results but also to some extent subjective. Three years after the initial work David Croom invited Newell and Sorrell to carry out an audit - this was an opportunity to assess how effective the identity had been and to make any changes that might be needed.

We found a company that was now fiercely proud of its identity. In pure facts and figures some encouraging progress had been made. Routledge had jumped from number three to number one in its market. Sales had increased by a third in three years, and exports had grown significantly as a proportion, helping Routledge to beat the recession.

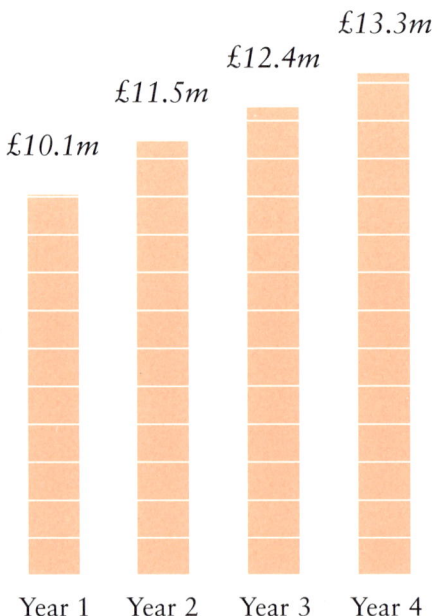

£10.1m   £11.5m   £12.4m   £13.3m

Year 1   Year 2   Year 3   Year 4

**Routledge sales since
the introduction of the new identity**

Outside the company, authors and booksellers recognised Routledge's strength. With hardly any advertising Routledge was perceived as a growing, dynamic force in academic publishing. David Croom pointed to improved motivation of the sales force and better marketing tools, all enhanced by the identity which remained the only new element in the company's operation.

Internally the story was equally positive. As David Croom explains, "One of the most important issues in integrating four imprints into a single new business was convincing all our staff that the new business had an identity and culture of its own. The visual identity played a major part in achieving that integration."

The company's design manager, Jo Hart, expresses an inside view : "The identity has been a resounding success. Remember that the publishing business is full of 'anarchists'. The identity was important in bringing everyone together, making everyone feel part of the same company."

In the two years following the introduction of the identity, figures for net sales per employee grew by 8 per cent and 14 per cent. Significant cost savings were also achieved by reorganising Routledge's design department to carry out a greater proportion of design in-house. At least

£100 of design costs were saved per jacket, but perhaps the increase in job satisfaction and design quality were even more significant.

Overall, I remain proud of what we were able to achieve by sharing and delivering Routledge's objectives. A disparate organisation gained focus, improved its operational performance and developed a distinctive visual style that delivers real commercial results.

And, as for myself, *I still love books.*

Key facts

In the three years after the introduction of
the new identity:

* Routledge climbed from number 3 to number 1
  in its market
* Sales increased by one third to £13.3 million,
  with annual increases of 14, 8 and 7%, leading
  to good profit levels.
* Exports increased significantly as a proportion
  of total sales
* Staff productivity and morale rose - and staff
  turnover reduced

**WINNER Design Effectiveness Award
for Corporate Identity**

*"This is an investment that has paid off.
Design has been the crucial factor, the asset which
has given Routledge visibility and has conveyed
a sense of our size."*

David Croom *Managing Director* Routledge

Unlocking innovation

by John Sorrell

Berol was known in the UK as a supplier of straightforward products to commercial markets - pens, pencils, markers. Newell and Sorrell's creation of innovative products and a new premium brand, Karisma, helped Berol break into the quality art-graphics market and open the way for expansion across Europe.

I have always believed that the more we learn about our clients the more we can help them.

Berol had been Newell and Sorrell's first client and we had learnt a lot about their products and their markets. The more we learnt, the better we could apply the knowledge we gained to Berol's advantage.

We had been working with Berol UK for some time when we were asked by Denis Thomas, President of Berol Corporation in the USA, to advise on the application of

Berol's corporate and brand identities in the different countries where it was based around the world. We visited factories and retail outlets in the USA, Canada, Venezuela, Mexico and Colombia, adding to our knowledge.

What we saw on our visits was the most curious metamorphosis of a product and brand unknown in the UK, called Prismacolor. In Colombia, for example, the sign above the Bogota factory said Prismacolor, not Berol - Prismacolor was a colour pencil selling in enormous quantities to all ages and across all markets, commercial, educational and artistic. Its presentation was cheerful, gaudy, unsophisticated.

Other visits followed to other countries. The further north we went in America - from Mexico, to the USA, to Canada - the greater the sense of exclusivity surrounding the Prismacolor product. In New York, in the Museum of Modern Art, we saw works hanging with the accompanying description 'Drawn with Prismacolor'.

So here was a world-class product, marketed under a brand which stood for different values in every different market. "What if we brought the product to Europe and created a brand around it?"

We planted the thought in our report to Berol, and eventually the thought grew and saw the light of day.

Three main obstacles had to be overcome.

First, although Berol had been making and selling 'graphic' products for years - pens, pencils, art materials - these were commodity products sold in the main to commercial stationery and educational markets. Berol was only on the periphery of the art materials and graphics markets in the UK and Europe. *Second*, for legal reasons, Berol could not use the Prismacolor name or brand in Europe. And *third*, as Roger Young, Berol's marketing manager rightly said, "There are enough coloured pencils to satisfy the world until Armageddon."

Our own research made it clear that Berol had little or no reputation in an intensely competitive market which features some well-known brands; also that the market was more quality-conscious than price-conscious, and not influenced by short-term fashion trends.

But there was obvious potential for a high quality innovative product range which combined superb performance with unique positioning. Berol's new brand proposition needed to be, above all, about differentiation.

We developed a strategy capable of driving a wedge into the professional art-graphics market with a new brand and innovative new products. The objective was to achieve a significant market share in three years.

Several key decisions were made. We would leapfrog the competition by differentiating the brand to position it at the top of the market. We would use coloured pencils as the flagship product. We would create distinctive product features. We would create a new name - Karisma. We would present the products in unique packaging.

But a pencil is a pencil is a pencil - how do you differentiate such a mundane commodity?

We started with the pencil itself. Instead of applying coats of coloured lacquer to the pencils we kept them in their natural wood finish, protected with a coat of clear varnish. One end of the pencil was sharpened and the other was given a unique 'chamfer'. This not only provided a completely unique product in terms of looks, it also gave the user the benefit of seeing the exact lead colour at both ends. At a stroke, Karisma pencils were different from anything else in the market. At the same time, these simple products became elegant, stylish and appropriate. We followed the theme of appropriateness with the packaging.

Materials were chosen to reflect the traditional qualities of the pencil, with special papers and brass eyelet details designed to reflect timeless values. Hallmarks were developed to suggest the idea of quality, collectability and exclusiveness to users.

The first new Karisma pencil product to reach the market was a graphite aquarelle, in early 1987. Its task was to build awareness for the brand. Its quality and unusual presentation quickly attracted attention, laying the ground for the successful launch of the Karisma colour pencils a few months later.

Both products were endorsed by leading artists whose work was featured in promotional material. Technically they were not 'new' products as such - the leads were already being widely used in Prismacolor products around the world. What was new was their availability for the first time in the UK, their elegant product presentation, and the quiet distinctiveness of the packaging and brand identity.

By 1988 when the third Karisma product - a set of double-ended markers - was introduced, Berol UK had a success on its hands. From a standing start with zero sales, Karisma became a £1 million brand with sales right across Europe in just five years.

Sales roughly doubled every year in this period as Italy, Holland, Belgium and Scandinavia became important markets as well as the UK. Volume growth was as encouraging as it was consistent. Distribution was achieved through more than 700 new outlets. Original sales estimates were exceeded by 60 per cent.

"Karisma became the flagship product range which enabled Berol to sell other products under its wing," said Howard James, Berol's international marketing director. "Our export people used it as a spearhead for growth in European markets. The brand grew at an astonishing rate."

Roger Young, like any marketing manager, had been under some pressure to justify his investment in creating the brand. In the event, the investment was repaid within the first year rather than the three-year payback that had been budgeted for.

Berol UK's marketing director at the time, Jeff Evans, explained what the launch of Karisma meant to the company - "more jobs, more turnover, increased distribution, and high credibility in the graphics market."

Today, Berol products sell in countries where they were unknown before Karisma was developed. The significance of this innovation came home to me a while ago when I was store-checking in New York. In art-graphics stores there I saw Karisma colour pencils selling alongside Prismacolor - with Karisma selling *at twice the price.*

Key facts

The creation of the Karisma brand and product innovations achieved:

* Steady year-on-year doubling of sales over five years, exceeding forecasts by 60%

* Annual sales of £1 million within five years of the launch

* Design investment payback within one year, not three years as budgeted

* New outlets opened in European export markets

"Newell and Sorrell's creation of the Karisma brand proved a major key to opening new distribution channels, particularly in export markets. It made us very conscious of how powerful design can be in the marketing process"

Roger Young *Marketing Manager*
Berol UK

"It's agreed then, we'll name him Rex and keep him"

Something to smile about

by *Tony Allen*

How could any company with the opportunity facing WHSmith not go for it? They did, and with the help of design as a catalyst to drive their business forward, WHSmith Business Supplies positioned itself to reap real benefits.

The UK office supplies market covers everything you would expect to find in an office, from computers to rubber bands. It's a substantial yet relatively undynamic market that hasn't seen much change since the mid 70's when the idea of single source supply arrived from America (the idea that you could buy everything you need from one supplier including furniture, stationery, computers, the lot). To be honest, you could say it lacked excitement and humour.

Certainly one of the reasons for its lack of dynamism is its sales-driven nature, and like many big commodity markets, office supplies chugs along with the same old players constantly slugging it out on price for the biggest office contracts. There aren't many laughs around when '2 for the price of 1' or '20% off' are regarded as creative concepts.

In 1988 WHSmith emerged on the scene, keen to exploit possible synergies between its high street retail business and its new emerging office supplies business. The Group purchased six of the then leading contract stationers which were quickly abbreviated to five, leaving Cartwright Brice, Chapmans, Sandhurst, Satex and Pentagon. WHSmith then set up a controlling company, WHSmith Business Supplies, to manage the five formerly competitor companies as one group. Not an easy task by anyone's standards, but WHSmith Business Supplies in one fell swoop had become the largest contract supply group in the UK. And with its size came the lucrative economies of scale which it would use to great advantage later on.

Newell and Sorrell also entered the picture in 1989 shortly after the acquisition by WHSmith of the six companies.

The original brief was to create a brand identity to tie together four sub-ranges into one large own brand range which would be offered by each of the companies in the group.

The strategy at this stage was quite clear - by bringing together the individual strengths of the five businesses, WHSmith Business Supplies would be able to outperform other competitors in many different areas. Notably, there was the greater economy of scale achieved through centralised buying, and the benefits from this which could be passed on to WHSmith's customers.

Newell and Sorrell began its programme with research and analysis. What emerged from this led eventually to a much bigger idea than had previously been imagined. Our research threw up the usual findings: a commodity style market place, populated by established but conservative buyers whose jobs were to get the best price out of contract stationery suppliers. But there were also some new findings.

In some companies, we saw that the old style office stationery buyer had been replaced by a multi-disciplined manager who took responsibility for a variety of infrastructure resources, including office stationery. With the new manager's role, we identified greater sophistication and the requirement for his or her suppliers also to provide a more sophisticated product and service.

This reason helped reinforce discussions which led to the recommendation that WHSmith had to think very seriously about redefining its position - in fact, to use its dominant size to redefine the way the market viewed office supplies. Our proposal developed. We recommended that WHSmith adopt a new visual identity which would communicate a unique idea in much more depth than simply a new range of own brand packaging. This thinking helped us to create the values and positioning for what later became the Niceday brand from WHSmith Business Supplies.

The vehicle - through which we communicated the idea of the new business - was *humour*. Newell and Sorrell created a visual identity comprising many elements which had, at its heart, the idea of playful drawings by Charley Barsotti, the American cartoonist.

Together, we created the Niceday pup, the 'spokesman' for the new identity.

The new visual identity was introduced to packaging for over 2000 different products and in each case the pup or the other Niceday characters (a bird and worm) interacts with the Niceday logo to create a visual pun.

The idea was to challenge continually the kind of stuffy and bureaucratic conventions which everyone sees in offices. By using humour as an entry point, Niceday could create an expectation that everything it did would have a human, warm and accessible face.

So, as a result the tone of voice, language and service style always tries to be as simple and direct as possible. The new identity was launched in September 1992 and phased in over a six month period across all faces of the new business.

The results of the introduction of Niceday swiftly brought a smile to the face of senior WHSmith executives. In a period where the total office supplies market grew by only 1 per cent to £3.7 billion, the WHSmith Business Supplies' sales between 1992 and 1994 increased by 19 per cent to £154 million.

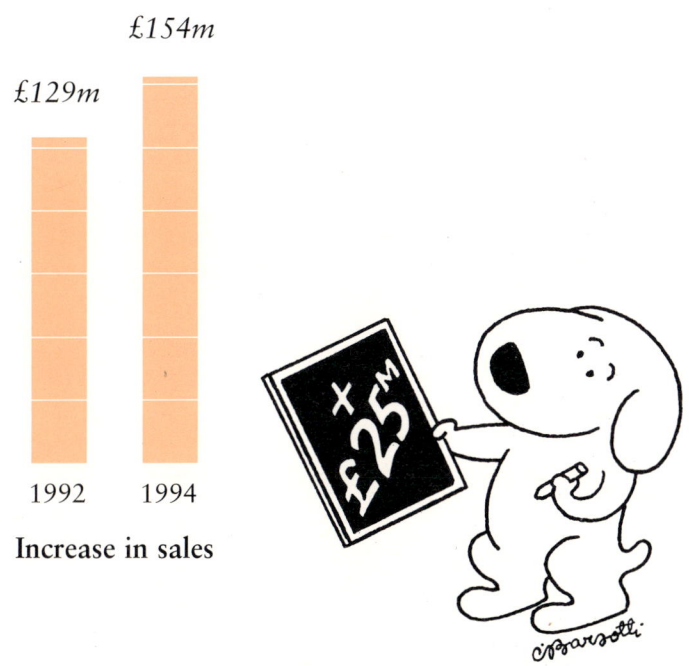

£154m

£129m

1992   1994

Increase in sales

Research revealed that the new image had a positive effect on internal and customer morale. Buying office supplies was no longer a dreary stress purchase. As one customer explained, "The cartoons cheer up the products - they make you smile automatically." Until April 1994, when a national press and direct mail campaign broke and the Niceday dog featured on 300 poster sites in the south-east, advertising of the Niceday brand was limited to the trade press. PR activity was similarly restricted to the trade press, reinforcing the conclusion that the visual identity was the key differentiating factor in uniting a disparate group of businesses and boosting sales, profits and market share.

And the fax lines between London and Kansas, where Charley Barsotti lives and works, remain hot. Receiving an overnight cartoon by fax from Charley is always a good way to start the day. *But that's another, funny story ...*

Key facts

The launch of Niceday resulted in:

* A 19% increase in sales

* Sales increase achieved in a total market which grew by only 1%

* A dramatic change in customer perceptions of office products

WINNER Design Effectiveness Award for Corporate Identity

"Newell and Sorrell worked hard to see that the idea they had created could eventually influence all aspects of our business for the better. Our customers have seen these positive changes and, as a result, our sales have improved substantially."

Donald Kerr *Chief Executive*
WHSmith Business Supplies

All change

by Iain MacTavish

From heavy loss-maker to the world's first national passenger rail operator to make a profit, InterCity's turnaround in the late 1980s was a triumph of quality and design. A new identity, designed to make it the flagship brand in British Rail, proved to be a catalyst for change.

The days are long gone when every boy wanted to be a train driver, but a little bit of the romance of trains lingers on. Especially when you're travelling in comfort at over 100 miles an hour through the countryside. That is the experience of InterCity that we had to capture and convey to those who love trains and those who do not.

Dr John Prideaux used to begin speeches by stating "I love trains". Soon after he was appointed Director of InterCity, Newell and Sorrell were brought on board. It was

1986 and InterCity had been set a formidable challenge. Losses were running at £125 million a year and the Government announced that InterCity would be required to make a profit in four years' time. Not only that, all subsidies would be phased out in two years. At that time no national, long distance passenger railway in the world operated at a profit.

It was as if the train announcement had been made: "All change, please!" InterCity needed an identity that would signal the change to customers and the need for change to its internal audiences in British Rail. The new identity would inevitably be aspirational, but it would be the glue linking the three tenets of InterCity's turnaround strategy - quality, efficiency and growth.

British Rail was at that time divided into five businesses : InterCity, Network South East, Provincial, Parcels and Freight. The businesses were not much loved by the public, indeed they were often the subjects of jokes rather than admiration. InterCity itself had never been perceived or presented as a proper brand. "InterCity was seen as a label but no more," said John Prideaux. "We needed to build the InterCity identity."

The commercial reasons driving this were clear. InterCity had to turn loss into profit. It also had to turn customer indifference, at best, into affection - and staff cynicism into loyalty. The emphasis in the strategy was clearly on quality, supported by efficiency, leading to growth. Raising the standard of InterCity service was crucial in a marketplace where the train could never be the cheapest option. The new identity had to make clear the commitment to quality, it had to show InterCity as the flagship brand of British Rail.

In truth, things started from a very low base. InterCity seemed inextricably linked to British Rail's curled-up sandwiches. Even the logotype for InterCity used the same typography as station signs for *Way Out* and *Toilets*.

It was always going to be a long haul because InterCity had to travel such a long way in its own self-regard as well as in the public's perception. We knew that there would be no massive capital investment to transform the railway overnight. We needed to make a virtue of necessity, creating an identity that would work hard within tight constraints.

The basic elements of the identity have, therefore, a practical, engineered character. The silver swallow emblem was an important element in summing up this character. It became a hallmark of quality, gaining symbolic meaning as part of the drive to raise standards - staff had to earn the silver swallow badge.

Similar thinking was applied to the introduction of the identity on InterCity trains, making a positive attribute of the economic fact that InterCity could only afford to apply the identity when equipment was renewed or refurbished. This meant that it took six years for the traction and rolling stock to be upgraded and for the identity to be applied to this new or overhauled equipment. It also meant that the identity became a clear badge of quality and a source of pride linked to the visible achievement of higher standards.

This thinking applied to every area of InterCity's business. The identity was used, deliberately, as a catalyst for change. With the identity we were able to plant a flag some way in the distance and realistically expect people to reach it.

For example, we brought all the InterCity managers together at a conference and involved them in the principles of *success through quality*. This was a unifying act of communication and motivation never before experienced by InterCity people.

There were many other examples. We designed a *Fact File* which helped InterCity talk to its business audiences through a positioning publication serving a similar role to an annual report. We created a map which communicated the truly national scope of the network in a symbolic way as well as providing clear route information.

We saw people struggling to carry food and drink from the buffet to their seats, and we also observed that they then had nowhere to tidy away their litter. The carrier bag we introduced met both needs. It also paid for itself because the bag could become an advertising medium and the space could be sold.

In time, and through a strong design management system that we operated with InterCity, the identity reached into every area of the business. As well as train livery and coach interiors, areas such as on-board services, uniforms, signs, literature and publicity, communications and environments have all been developed in line with the fundamental design strategy. A vast number of small changes added up to an achievement of great significance. The change was palpable and, indeed, it was measurable in facts and figures.

Following the initiation of the identity programme, InterCity turned from a loss-maker to a profitable business. Losses of £125 million in 1986 were turned into profits of £57 million by 1989, a year ahead of target. InterCity became the world's only national passenger railway to run at a profit. Nor was this a one-off. Profit levels were maintained in subsequent years. With a £1 billion turnover

InterCity became one of the top 150 businesses in the country and it had confidence in itself as a business.

That confidence has been tested in recent years with changes still coming thick and fast. The privatisation programme has led to uncertainty and the break-up of the unified network run by InterCity. Once the catalyst of change, the InterCity identity has now taken on a new role as a sign of stability and authority in the midst of confusing change. InterCity's value as a brand has been recognised in the balance sheet and it has now become an endorsement sought by new franchises. Indeed, the brand's success has convinced previously sceptical business people that railways can compete and can be run profitably.

The InterCity identity leaves a strong legacy of large and small achievements that mean a lot. A valuable brand where none existed previously. Sandwiches that are every bit as good as Marks & Spencer's. About a billion pounds worth of profits earned and public subsidy saved. And a much easier, safer way for you to carry your hot tea and biscuits on a fast-moving train - as well as leave the place tidy afterwards. *That, in itself, makes a change.*

Key facts:

The InterCity achievement:

* Losses of £125million in 1986 turned into profits of £57million by 1989 - one year ahead of target

* Continued profits since turnaround

* Fast traffic growth

* Increase of almost 70% in First Class sales (£95million to £161million)

* Raised customer expectations, changed customer attitudes

* It became the only long distance passenger railway in the world to operate at a profit without government subsidy

"Our relationship with Newell and Sorrell has been clearly successful - they have managed to get under our skin ... they understood the importance of the customer and our aspirations."

Dr John Prideaux *Director* InterCity

Breaking cover

by Rodney Mylius

Bloomsbury had four founders who knew about books; start-up capital to get them off the ground; and an identity created by Newell and Sorrell in the very first days of the company. Now Bloomsbury is the highest of high-profile publishers.

The first time I met the four people who were then Bloomsbury was in a tiny, shabby office above an estate agents in Putney. Very 1980s. But at least there were no pretensions. It meant that I liked them and that was important because for a designer, unlike for a doctor or a nurse, detachment can be a professional drawback. I believe design only counts when you *do* get involved.

Nigel Newton, David Reynolds, Alan Wherry and Liz Calder had plenty of ambition and enthusiasm. That much was obvious from the start but, more crucially for me, they had a real desire to create something fresh in the publishing world. At a time when the traditional publishing houses were merging or conglomerating into corporate giants, they planned to do the exact opposite. They were coming out of senior positions in firms like Penguin and Jonathan Cape and they stated their intent to challenge the old, accepted assumptions about the way to publish books.

I came with my own burning desires and convictions, based on my own recent experience of working in the very traditional Oxford University Press. I wanted to challenge the conventions of book design. It seemed like we had important aims in common.

Commercially, a crucial objective for Bloomsbury's design approach was to make the company and its books feel as if they had always been there. We all realised that if this was to be achieved the greatest mistake would be to pastiche familiar 'booky' styles. Bloomsbury would only look right if it had its own strong personality and branding, regardless of what the competition was doing.

For example, if you think about chocolate snack bars everyone is struggling to look like KitKat. Think about fizzy drinks and they all try to be Coca-Cola. But if Bloomsbury was to be a great publisher of hardback books, it could not be so by copying Faber & Faber.

The four founders had sold their ideas brilliantly to us, and the Bloomsbury look was based on capturing a sense of their vibrant personalities. Out of this, immediately, came the idea for the hand-drawn colophon which sprang out of Liz Calder's love for 'Diana the Huntress'. Bloomsbury, the hunter for new authors - also, in another of Diana's attributes, the midwife of creativity. The Bloomsbury logotype, hand-drawn using Eric Gill letters, followed soon after and we decided that the logotype should be displayed on the front jacket - "an act of corporate immodesty that was a tremendous success," according to Nigel Newton.

Most important of all was the book itself, the vehicle in which people entrust their most precious belongings - their words. How many great stories have sunk into oblivion over the years simply because they were presented in a package that failed to attract enough consumers?

For decades hardback books had been considered a declining product. Publishers and consumers seemed to share a belief that they were outdated and expensive compared to paperbacks. Yet the evidence suggested the opposite. From a time when hardbacks had been five times the price of a paperback, they were at this time about twice the price. Hardbacks were not really all that expensive, therefore, but their appearance did not give the impression of value because shortcuts in production had been taken over the years which had reduced the quality of the product. They seemed like paperbacks with harder covers.

By challenging and pushing production values all the time we soon discovered that we were able to add value to hardback books and to justify a higher price. It was not simply restoring to books the ribbon markers which all publishers had abandoned previously, but also insisting that each book should have special end papers, embossing, decorative title pages, considered typographic layouts and even a way to present the dreaded bar code as something more than a hammered-on necessity.

We asked more questions. We asked printers why the inside flaps of a jacket were so mean and small? There was no good reason, so we used bigger, full-page flaps to carry high-quality pictures of the authors. The authors, after all, were Bloomsbury's stars, and we reinforced this idea by blocking the author's initials and stars from the colophon onto the fabric of the cover.

In short, we looked at the design of Bloomsbury books not as an exercise in book design but as a piece of packaging design for a high quality product. Did it work? Perhaps the measure of Bloomsbury's success is that it now seems impossible to imagine the publishing world without them. Undoubtedly the book-buying public caught on, seeing Bloomsbury as the cavaliers and liking them for being seen to be different. We emphasised this by producing a wealth of material to market Bloomsbury itself. Nigel Newton identified these items as reinforcing Bloomsbury's prestige among authors: "I know that authors have been attracted to us by our high visibility and quality." Just look at the authors on Bloomsbury's list.

Did it work financially? In the three years following Bloomsbury's launch the company exceeded its targets, moving to an operating profit of £639,000 in its third year. Turnover rose from £2.2 million in 1987 to £7 million in 1989, a year universally described within the book trade as 'diabolical' for book publishers. A few years further on and Bloomsbury successfully floated on the Stock Exchange.

The fact was everyone always believed Bloomsbury was special. It created an aura around itself. If the authors were movie stars they should be published by a company as desirable and glamorous as a Hollywood movie studio. There was going to be a Bloomsbury way of doing things and the way this was manifested was through design. As the *Guardian* observed: "Bloomsbury is a new publishing house which promises to produce not only books of quality, but books worth owning."

The more rewarding aspect was discovering that, by upping the stakes with a bigger than usual bet on design, Bloomsbury managed to bring books to whole new audiences. Of course, traditional book shops responded well to having attractive products supported by a striking identity, and in launch week Charing Cross Road adopted Bloomsbury as its own. But more revealingly and notoriously, Paul Smith, the fashion designer, started selling Bloomsbury books in his shops.

Above all, the most rewarding aspect of working for Bloomsbury was knowing that this was a venture that would make a difference. Imitators, of course, followed on Bloomsbury's distinctive style of publishing but the fact remains that now, wherever I see a Bloomsbury book, I still pick it up because I think it will be worthwhile. Even if it is *Princess in love.*

Key facts

The corporate identity for Bloomsbury
Publishing led to:

* An exceptionally successful high-profile launch

* A rapid rise in turnover from £2.2 million in
  year one to £7 million in year three, with an
  operating profit of £639,000

* Sales of first novels 50% higher than the
  industry norm

* A solid foundation for future development,
  including flotation in 1994

Design Effectiveness Award Finalist

*"The identity gave our young company credibility,
helping us to establish ourselves incredibly quickly ...
I would estimate that design, as an isolated factor,
has led to a 20% increase in sales."*

Nigel Newton *Managing Director*
Bloomsbury Publishing

In touch with the future

by John Simmons

The art of letter-writing remains crucial to Royal Mail's business - which is why it runs an annual letter-writing competition to encourage the habit in young people. Newell and Sorrell's role - in writing and designing the promotional materials and the prize, LetterBox - has led to phenomenal increases in participation.

Design is about the future. It is about the future in many different ways. It allows us to see things and imagine what they will be like. It brings new ideas into being. It is supremely optimistic, because it is about making life.

All of these things are vital to me. I want to make the future better, not just for me, but for my children, and for all the children still to come.

The work Newell and Sorrell carries out in education is very important for me. I believe in it absolutely. This belief ensures that value is constantly being added - in the form of fresh ideas - to the educational programmes we undertake. This is particularly so with our work for Royal Mail.

People are often surprised that Royal Mail has such an extensive educational programme for schools and young people. But Royal Mail has been around for centuries, and if it is still to be around next century it needs to build the interest of future consumers in activities which are central to its existence. Letter-writing, for example.

There is a popular perception that letter-writing is a dying art - a social communication eroded by such technologies as telephone, fax and electronic mail. However, the reality is that levels of letter-writing have not declined over the past 15 years. Social mail still accounts for some 2.9 billion letters sent per year - a not insignificant 15 per cent of all letters delivered by Royal Mail. The pleasure of receiving a letter still makes people look forward to the post arriving - just in case.

Against this background, Royal Mail is understandably keen to encourage the habit of letter-writing in young people from an early age. Its annual letter-writing competition, aimed at school children from 4 to 16, is a key tool to achieving this.

The competition began in 1975 in a small-scale way, with the objective of encouraging letter-writing by children and raising its status as an educational activity among teachers. Numbers of entrants grew steadily but reached a plateau in the late 1980s.

In 1990, with the number of entries standing at a respectable but static 145,000, Royal Mail decided to reshape the competition in a bid to attract more schoolchildren. Instead of big prizes being awarded to only a handful of children who write the very best letters, it was decided to give a prize to every entrant.

Newell and Sorrell were commissioned to devise and design that prize. The following year we also took over the task of inventing the theme and designing all material related to the competition - as part of a new strategy to make the event more exciting and to reinforce its credibility in schools.

I think the expectation was that for the prize we would source a stationery gift that would carry Royal Mail branding. What seemed to us much more valuable was to create a branded printed product - LetterBox - to enhance Royal Mail's authority in the youth education market through links with letter-writing.

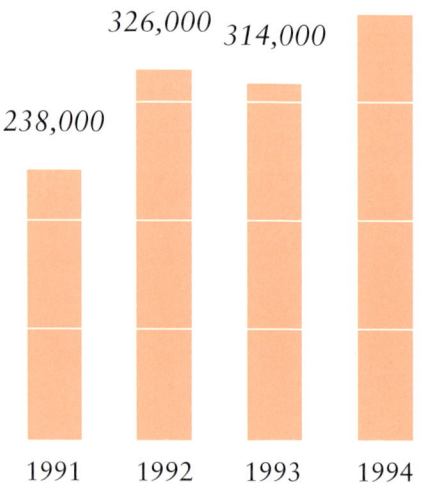

238,000   326,000   314,000   375,000

1991   1992   1993   1994

**Number of entrants to
the Young Letter-writers Competition**

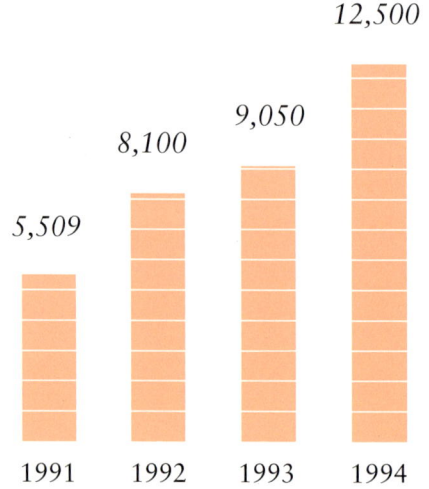

5,509   8,100   9,050   12,500

1991   1992   1993   1994

**Increase in teachers participating in
the competition since 1991**

The first competition theme we set, in 1992, was 'Green'. The following year it was 'Free', and in 1994 the theme was 'Peace'. Working with different illustrators we created a fresh, enticing style for each year's promotional material - poster, letter and leaflet - sent out to primary and secondary head teachers and heads of English.

But it is LetterBox that sets this competition apart. LetterBox makes sure that every child is a winner. LetterBox is like the Tardis - it is full of more than seems possible. Special effects such as multiple concertina folds, die-cuts and scratch-and-sniff convey a sense of fun and surprise which support the varied messages about writing contained in LetterBox.

In 1992 the LetterBox *Book of Letters* examined different angles on letter-writing through words about each letter of the alphabet. In 1993 the LetterBox *Bestiary*, or book of beasts, looked at ways of communicating and sending messages, taking animals as its point of reference. In 1994 the LetterBox *Herbarium*, or book of plants, explored the ways in which we draw inspiration and meaning from plants to send messages. Environmental issues provided the underlying theme for all three editions of LetterBox.

The effect on entries to the competition was dramatic. From a relatively high base of 238,000 entries in 1991, the first year of our involvement, entries leapt by 58 per cent to the 1994 figure of 375,000 in three years.

In the first year of the new competition format, entries rose by 88,000 or 37 per cent to 326,000, exceeding the target of 300,000 by 9 per cent.

These increases are put in context by study of some background data. According to 1991 Census figures, the total number of children aged between 5 and 16 in the UK is estimated to be 8.5 million. This means that, in 1994, the Royal Mail letter-writing competition attracted the support of 4.4 per cent of the total population in this age group. In certain age bands one in every eight children entered the competition.

Of course, few children would know about the competition if teachers did not use it as a classroom activity. It is vital, therefore, that teachers perceive the material as having educational credibility. From research carried out we know that teachers especially appreciate the competition theme being thought-provoking and stretching, capable of fitting into the established educational calendar and adaptable to the needs of the National Curriculum. Teachers recognise the value of writing a 'live' letter, and they appreciate the educational worth of LetterBox as well as understanding it as an incentive for children to participate. And, of course, year by year LetterBox builds the legend of itself among children receiving it, encouraging more entries in the following year.

In terms of cost effectiveness, it is estimated that taking into account all design fees, printing and distribution costs, the cost to Royal Mail per entry is less than £3. This means that if the competition encourages each child to send 12 first class letters in their lifetime, the event pays for itself.

But money aside, there is also the broader benefit to Royal Mail in being associated with a national event which encourages schoolchildren to think about their surroundings and respect the environment.

Right from the start LetterBox has had a 'green', campaigning theme, in keeping with the interests of its recipients. Through LetterBox (always produced with recycled materials) we have explored issues like endangered wildlife and disappearing rain forests, making links with the potential of letters to change the world.

The whole event is run without advertising. LetterBox is clearly the decisive factor in increasing competition entries and participation within education, as Kevin Doherty of Royal Mail acknowledged. "LetterBox has enabled Royal

Mail to communicate meaningfully with literally hundreds of thousands of children, their teachers and their parents. The competition is crucial to our long term role in the country's business life."

But, for me, what matters most of all is that we enfranchise young people and give them proper respect. A healthy society needs to encourage creativity, imagination and confidence among its future citizens. Through letter-writing we can help young people to think for themselves, to express their ideas and to believe that their voices can be heard. Jonathon Porritt, who was one of the judges for the 'Green' competition in 1992, said the following: "To have all those children writing letters with ideas on saving the earth - to see the piles of concern in the letters stacking up - was a moving experience. The children's letters gave me hope for the world."

I find it a satisfying postscript to add that *Letters of Peace*, a selection of letters from the 1994 competition, is now a book published by Pavilion. *So the children's voices have been heard.*

Key facts

* Entries to the letter-writing competition increased by 58% in three years

* Entries rose from 145,000 in 1990 to 375,000 in 1994

* Support by teachers increased by 126%

* A cost-effective investment in the consumers of the future

WINNER Design Effectiveness Award for Corporate Literature

WINNER Design Effectiveness Environmental Award

"LetterBox's real value to Royal Mail is as a unique differentiator. No one else can do this competition. No one else has the rationale. That makes it an invaluable asset to our brand."

Kevin Doherty
Director of consumer services Royal Mail

Choosing effective design

by *Simon Jones*

The whole notion of design effectiveness is still in its
infancy. This youngster will no doubt grow and, in years
to come, forget that I ever said anything to its benefit.

The problem is that we all mean different things by
'design'. For too many people - prejudiced by 'designer'
labels - design is a way to apply a cosmetic gloss to
something that lacks substance. And, no doubt, there is
design like that and designers who do just that. But we
need to move towards a new definition of design that
we can all share - or perhaps we need to re-establish or
re-emphasise an older meaning of design.

Ask yourself what you actually mean by 'design'. Design
is a broader church than you might first imagine and the
work described in this book - no apologies for this - is
distinguished by the fact that it is concerned with going far
below the decorative surface of a project. A decorative

finish is nice but that, by itself, is design that appeals and works on a very shallow level.

We have all been influenced by the fact that design has become a subject taught alongside art. Inevitably, therefore, design is judged by the way it looks. Design has to be a visual subject.

That's all very well but it is not completely true to the meaning of design. Look the word up in a dictionary and you will find not only definitions like 'a preliminary sketch for a work of art' and 'artistic idea as executed' but also 'a plan or scheme conceived in the mind of something to be done'. Design is about *thinking*.

So the only real rule in choosing effective design is to probe into the thinking. For any design consultancy that wants to be effective will start with a period of thinking. A good design consultant, you will find, is someone who always wants to learn.

Design, therefore, starts with questions. There is a nice story about a little boy learning sums in school.

Teacher: 'There are two cakes, one of which is sliced into thirds and the other into quarters. Which cake has the larger slices?'

The boy: 'How big is each cake?'

A consultancy such as Newell and Sorrell is made up of many individuals who all ask good questions and love to learn something new every day. Those individuals have idiosyncratic approaches and they bring different capabilities to crack problems and to spot opportunities.

Clients rarely have needs that are specific or narrow - they need a much broader and deeper approach. They need the range and depth of a multi-disciplined team.

The people who have written the case studies in this book are members as well as leaders of multi-disciplined teams. That is the way we do it and it is a model that other design consultancies have variants of. I think there is no getting away from the basic fact that design is a team game at its best. Each consultant at Newell and Sorrell is supported by a team, and if the case studies here are written by individuals - and their personalities are crucial to the effectiveness of a project - then it would be wrong to neglect the importance of the whole team. That team, stating the obvious, is also made up of individuals.

The chemistry of teams is fascinating and can do much to create work that is innovative and inspiring as well as effective. The work described here is the result of brilliant individuals using different skills within a team.

The examples of design effectiveness in this book have

great variety. Some are about making money, some about raising awareness, some about changing cultures and influencing behaviour. They are all different because the individuals are different and the teams are different. Yet they all have a common thread which links them and which is the starting point for their success.

Establishing objectives is the starting point for creating effective design. These objectives may not be entirely clear to a client before a project starts but effective design consultants will prefer to explore and refine a brief as they work on it.

For a client, therefore, the important part of the selection and commissioning process is about exploring the design consultancy's ability to understand and formulate objectives - to assess the consultant's ability to think strategically because design is an analytical as well as a creative process. It follows from this that you do not choose effective design by giving a consultant a tiny amount of time and even less money to come up with some pictures in a 'pitch'. That is to miss the point of design consultancy altogether.

Remember that design is about thinking.

Design consultants will think in ways that are different from management consultants. There is a creative slant to the thinking. Design consultants often think about the same issues as management consultants, but produce more imaginative solutions which enable companies to leap ahead. But, as this book shows, design consultancy can be as hard-nosed, practical and commercial as any other business resource.

So my final advice is to be as open-minded as you can about design. Do not put design into a neat pigeonhole - design, in any case, has a tendency to burst out of constraints put upon it. Treat design seriously, put your faith in it but make demands of it. Seek a quality of thinking that goes beneath a shallow sheen. *And choose the best people.*

About the Authors

John Sorrell is co-chairman of Newell and Sorrell and has led an enormous number of design and consultancy projects throughout his career. John is a regular speaker on design matters, corporate identity and corporate communications, chairing and speaking at numerous conferences and appearing on TV and radio. He gave the inaugural lecture of the new corporate identity course at the Elisava School of Design at Barcelona University and spoke on Corporate Vision at the Third International Design Forum in Singapore. He chaired the Indo-British Partnership seminar 'Designing to win in World Markets' in New Delhi, organised as part of the recent DTI trade mission to India. An active member of the design community for thirty years, John's former design industry appointments include Chairman of the Design Business Association, a Vice-President of the Chartered Society of Designers and a member of the Industry Lead Body for Design. John became Chairman of the Design Council in January 1994. He is the first designer to be Chairman.

Frances Newell co-chairs and is design director of Newell and Sorrell, leading programmes which have won many awards for creativity and design effectiveness in the UK, Europe and the USA. These include three silver D&AD Awards, six DBA Design Effectiveness Awards, two Art Directors Club of Europe Awards, three Gold New York Festivals Medals, two gold and three silver Clios and the Eurobest Award. She is a Fellow of the Chartered Society of Designers, a Fellow of the Royal Society of Arts and a member of the Colour Group. She has judged the Royal Society of Art's student awards, the Designers and Art Directors Association Awards, the Royal Academy/Royal Mail Young Artists competition and the BBC TV Design Awards. She currently chairs the City and Guilds National Advisory Committee for Craft, Design and Art.

Jeremy Scholfield is a director of Newell and Sorrell and heads up the specialist branding and packaging team. Originally a design graduate, Jeremy is a skilled manager of design and has been responsible for Newell and Sorrell's work with Boots since 1988, working with five Business Centres. He has directed projects for Coca Cola, Del Monte, Wella, Halfords, Bristol Myers and WHSmith. Many of these projects have won awards in Europe and the USA including two Clios and an International Global Award. He is a regular speaker on branding and design issues, and last year returned to his old school, Charterhouse, to deliver a lecture on brand identity in the UK. He recently became a father, a role for which his work with Boots had given him extensive preparation.

John Simmons is a director of Newell and Sorrell. He has a degree in English Literature from Oxford University. He worked extensively in publishing as an editor and copywriter and as Communications Manager at the National Economic Development Office before joining Newell and Sorrell in 1984. Since then he has been responsible for many major identity and communications programmes, including those for the Royal Mail and Waterstone's. He has run writing workshops for International Thomson, Routledge and WHSmith, and was a speaker at the 'Design means business' conference in Hong Kong. He was a judge in 1994 of the British Environment and Media Awards. John was a member of the Design Council's Primary Education Advisory Group and is a Trustee of the educational charity Art & Society and a Fellow of the Royal Society of Arts. His book *The Trouble with Words* was published in 1993.

Tony Allen is managing director of Newell and Sorrell's international business in the Netherlands. He read physical anthropology at Cambridge University before joining McCann Erikson London to work on international advertising accounts. In 1985 he joined Newell and Sorrell where his main area of activity has been corporate and brand identity programmes for clients in the UK, USA and mainland Europe including Cadbury Schweppes, Rabobank, Niceday, Union Railways, Waitrose and Ferrosan. Tony was a delegate on the Duke of Edinburgh's Seventh Commonwealth Study Conference held last year in thirteen regional centres around the UK. He is a lecturer on management and design with BTEC and has given talks on identity at client locations and the Strategic Planning Society in London.

Iain MacTavish joined Newell and Sorrell in 1982 from a background in advertising and marketing and is a director of the company. At Newell and Sorrell Iain has had wide experience in managing large identity and communications programmes for organisations such as BAA, InterCity, Parcelforce, Post Office Counters and the AA. He has a strong practical knowledge of the process and, particularly, the implementation and management of identity programmes. He has also been extensively involved in vehicle livery design having been responsible for projects for the Automobile Association, BAA and British Caledonian. His wide experience of transportation issues has been reinforced by several years of living on a narrow boat.

Rodney Mylius studied Graphic Design at Norwich School of Art, graduating in 1981. He joined Oxford University Press where he worked as an art director and later moved to Newell and Sorrell in 1985. Rodney has designed many projects including those for Bloomsbury, Grumbacher USA, Virago, THE, Waitrose and InterCity. From 1992 until April 1994, Rodney took a sabbatical from the company to take up an appointment as Professor of Visual Communications at the University of Tsukuba, Ibarki. During his period in Japan, he was awarded merit prizes in several competitions including that of the Tokyo Type Directors' Club. Rodney's relationship with the University has continued upon his return to Newell and Sorrell. Rodney has written many articles on aspects of design and communication for magazines including *baseline* and *Creative Review*.

Simon Jones is managing director of Newell and Sorrell. He started his career in advertising and for some 17 years worked at agencies such as Doyle Dane Bernbach, Saatchi & Saatchi and Lowe Howard Spink, before moving into identity consultancy in 1986 when he set up the London office of an American company. At Newell and Sorrell since 1990 Simon has been closely associated with programmes for the Automobile Association and Rabobank in Holland. He is a regular speaker on communications issues and related topics. Recently, he was a lecturer at the Duke of Edinburgh's Commonwealth Conference, and at the Institute of Management, with an address snappily entitled *"The role and impact of identity, culture, values and business ethics on organisations."*